OUT of the DEPTHS

RELATED BOOKS FROM
SAM TORODE BOOK ARTS

TAO TE CHING:
THE BOOK OF THE WAY
Lao Tzu

THE MANUAL:
A PHILOSOPHER'S GUIDE TO LIFE
Epictetus

THE MEDITATIONS:
AN EMPEROR'S GUIDE TO MASTERY
Marcus Aurelius

EVERYDAY EMERSON:
PATHBREAKING LECTURES
Ralph Waldo Emerson

AS A MAN THINKETH:
21ST CENTURY EDITION
James Allen

OUT *of the* DEPTHS

THE WAY THROUGH SORROW

OSCAR WILDE

edited and introduced by
SAM TORODE

Published by Sam Torode Book Arts

The elements unique to this book are
Copyright © 2018 Sam Torode.

Cover and interior photos of statues by Mammuth,
courtesy iStock Photo.

See related titles at:
www.amazon.com/author/samtorode

Connect on Facebook:
www.facebook.com/SamTorodeBooks

Facing page: Oscar Wilde's cell in Reading Gaol.

There is no prison into which love cannot force an entrance.
—Oscar Wilde

INTRODUCTION

In 1895, at the height of his literary success—immediately after his sparkling, brilliant comedy *The Importance of Being Earnest* premiered on the London stage—Oscar Wilde became embroiled in a legal case that ultimately exposed his homosexual double life, including dalliances with male prostitutes. He was convicted of gross indecency and sentenced to two years of hard labor. In the span of just a few months, Wilde went from social darling to public pariah—as dramatic a fall as anyone has ever experienced.

After stints in Pentonville and Wandsworth prisons, he was transferred to Reading Gaol ("gaol" being the archaic spelling of "jail"). His body broken by the harsh conditions, Wilde was deeply depressed. At Reading Gaol, a new, more sympathetic warden allowed Wilde to read—even loaning him books from his personal library—and, in the final months of his sentence, to write

INTRODUCTION

letters to his friends (though he was limited to writing one page per day).

He chose to write one long letter addressed to his former lover, Lord Alfred "Bosie" Douglas.

In the letter (the core of which forms the content of this book), Wilde processes his past and takes responsibility for the course of his life. In gut-wrenching yet exquisite prose, he expresses his humiliation, despair, suffering, and sorrow, and elucidates what he's learned from his descent into the shadow side of life. He then gives a unique, personal interpretation of the words and deeds of Jesus Christ. For Wilde, Jesus is an artist who made his entire life a poem, with the beauty of sorrow as its theme. In closing, Wilde further reflects on the relationship between art and sorrow, laying a new foundation for his own work going forward.

Wilde carried the letter with him upon release, and entrusted it to his friend (and, later, literary executor) Robert Ross. Though Wilde continued to write (most notably a long poem, "The Ballad of Reading Gaol"), he never recovered from the toll that prison took on his health, and he died in 1900—just three years after his release.

Several years after Wilde's death, Ross arranged for the publication of an abridged version of the prison letter—minus all references to Bosie—under the title *De Profundis* (Latin for "out of the depths," the opening words of Psalm 130).

Although the complete, unedited text of Wilde's letter was eventually published in 1962, I find Ross's abridged version more powerful than the original. Leaving out passages that are strictly personal and private, what remains is a universal statement of great interest—and potentially of great help—to all who must walk through the valley of sorrows.

For the present edition, I've taken Ross's version and made additional minor edits (primarily adding section breaks and smoothing a few transitions). I've also restored the original concluding paragraphs, which Ross left out.

Oscar Wilde's letter is the most profound account of sorrow and suffering that I've ever read. He charts the way *through* sorrow—not around it. We have to take responsibility for our lives—owning our own actions as well as the circumstances that are dealt to us—in order to take charge of our futures. "To regret one's own experiences," Wide says, "is to arrest one's development."

If we respond to suffering with love and acceptance instead of hate and bitterness, we will turn it to our benefit—just as nature turns waste and decay into fertile soil for new life. Wilde teaches us the alchemy by which anguish can be transmuted into empathy and art.

Today, with depression and despair afflicting so many—particularly creative and sensitive people—Wilde's letter is more relevant than ever. In publishing this new edition, I hope to cast light on a hidden gem that has the power to help us find meaning in our sorrows, and so to heal.

—Sam Torode

*Out of the depths have I cried
unto thee, O Lord.*
—Psalm 130

Suffering is one very long moment. We cannot divide it by seasons. We can only record its moods, and chronicle their return. With us time itself does not progress. It revolves. It seems to circle round one centre of pain. The paralyzing immobility of a life every circumstance of which is regulated after an unchangeable pattern, so that we eat and drink and lie down and pray, or kneel at least for prayer, according to the inflexible laws of an iron formula: this immobile quality, that makes each dreadful day in the very minutest detail like its brother, seems to communicate itself to those external forces the very essence of whose existence is ceaseless change. Of seed-time or harvest, of the reapers bending over the corn, or the grape gatherers threading through the vines, of the grass in the orchard made white with broken blossoms or strewn with fallen fruit: of these we know nothing and can know nothing.

For us there is only one season, the season of sorrow. The very sun and moon seem taken from us. Outside, the day may be blue and gold, but the light that creeps down through the thickly-muffled glass of the small iron-barred window beneath which one sits is grey and niggard. It is always twilight in one's cell, as it is always twilight in one's heart. And in the sphere of thought, no less than in the sphere of time, motion is no more.

A week after I was transferred to Reading Gaol, my mother died. No one knew how deeply I loved and honored her. Her death was terrible to me; but I, once a lord of language, have no words in which to express my anguish and my shame. She and my father had bequeathed me a name they had made noble and honored, not merely in literature, art, archaeology, and science, but in the public history of my own country, in its evolution as a nation. I had disgraced that name eternally. I had made it a low by-word among low people. I had dragged it through the very mire. I had given it to brutes that they might make it brutal, and to fools that they might turn it into a synonym for folly. What I suffered then, and still suffer, is not for pen to write or paper to record. My wife, always kind and gentle to me, rather than that I should hear the news from indifferent lips, travelled, ill as she was, all the way from Genoa to England to break to me herself the tidings of so irreparable, so irremediable, a loss. Messages of sympathy reached me from all who had still affection for me. Even people who had not known me personally, hearing that a new sorrow had broken into my life, wrote to ask that some expression of their condolence should be conveyed to me.

Three months have passed since my mother's death. The calendar of my daily conduct and labour that hangs on the outside of my cell door, with my name and sentence written upon it, tells me that it is May.

> *I, once a lord of language, have no words in which to express my anguish and my shame.*

PROSPERITY, pleasure and success, may be rough of grain and common in fibre, but sorrow is the most sensitive of all created things. There is nothing that stirs in the whole world of thought to which sorrow does not vibrate in terrible and exquisite pulsation. The thin beaten-out leaf of tremulous gold that chronicles the direction of forces the eye cannot see is in comparison coarse. It is a wound that bleeds when any hand but that of love touches it, and even then must bleed again, though not in pain.

Where there is sorrow there is holy ground. Some day people will realize what that means. They will know nothing of life till they do. Robbie [Robert Reed], and natures like his, can realize it. When I was brought down from my prison to the Court of Bankruptcy, between two policemen, Robbie waited in the long dreary corridor that, before the whole crowd, whom an action so sweet and simple hushed into silence, he might gravely raise his hat to me, as, handcuffed and with bowed head, I passed him by. Men have gone to heaven for smaller things than that. It was in this spirit, and with this mode of love, that the saints knelt down to wash the feet of the poor, or stooped to kiss the leper on the cheek. I have never said one single word to him about what he did. I do not know to the present moment whether he is aware that I was even conscious of his action. It is not a thing for which one can render formal thanks in formal words. I store it in the treasure-house of my heart. I keep it there as a secret debt that I am glad to think I can never possibly

> *Where there is sorrow there is holy ground.*

repay. It is embalmed and kept sweet by the myrrh and cassia of many tears. When wisdom has been profitless to me, philosophy barren, and the proverbs and phrases of those who have sought to give me consolation as dust and ashes in my mouth, the memory of that little, lovely, silent act of love has unsealed for me all the wells of pity: made the desert blossom like a rose, and brought me out of the bitterness of lonely exile into harmony with the wounded, broken, and great heart of the world. When people are able to understand, not merely how beautiful his action was, but why it meant so much to me, and always will mean so much, then, perhaps, they will realize how and in what spirit they should approach me.

THE poor are wise, more charitable, more kind, more sensitive than we are. In their eyes prison is a tragedy in a man's life, a misfortune, a casualty, something that calls for sympathy in others. They speak of one who is in prison as of one who is 'in trouble' simply. It is the phrase they always use, and the expression has the perfect wisdom of love in it. With people of our own rank it is different. With us, prison makes a man a pariah. I, and such as I am, have hardly any right to air and sun. Our presence taints the pleasures of others.

We are unwelcome when we reappear. To revisit the glimpses of the moon is not for us. Our very children are taken away. Those lovely links with humanity are broken. We are doomed to be solitary, while our sons still live. We are denied the one thing that might heal us and keep us, that might bring balm to the bruised heart, and peace to the soul in pain.

I must say to myself that I ruined myself, and that nobody great or small can be ruined except by his own hand. I am quite ready to say so. I am trying to say so, though they may not think it at the present moment. This pitiless indictment I bring without pity against myself. Terrible as was what the world did to me, what I did to myself was far more terrible still.

I was a man who stood in symbolic relations to the art and culture of my age. I had realized this for myself at the very dawn of my manhood, and had forced my age to realize it afterwards. Few men hold such a position in their own lifetime, and have it so acknowledged. It is usually discerned, if discerned at all, by the historian, or the critic, long after both the man and his age have passed away. With me it was different. I felt it myself, and made others feel it. Byron was a symbolic figure, but his relations were to the passion of his age and its weariness of passion. Mine were to something more noble, more permanent, of more vital issue, of larger scope.

The gods had given me almost everything. But I let myself be lured into long spells of senseless and sensual ease. I amused myself with being a *flâneur*, a dandy, a man of fashion. I surrounded myself with the smaller natures and the meaner minds. I became the spendthrift of my own genius, and to waste an eternal youth gave me a curious joy.

> *Terrible as was what the world did to me, what I did to myself was far more terrible still.*

Tired of being on the heights, I deliberately went to the depths in the search for new sensation. What the paradox was to me in the sphere of thought, perversity became to me in the sphere of passion. Desire, at the end, was a malady, or a madness, or both. I grew careless of the lives of others. I took pleasure where it pleased me, and passed on. I forgot that every little action of the common day makes or unmakes character, and that therefore what one has done in the secret chamber one has some day to cry aloud on the housetop. I ceased to be lord over myself. I was no longer the captain of my soul, and did not know it. I allowed pleasure to dominate me. I ended in horrible disgrace. There is only one thing for me now, absolute humility.

I have lain in prison for nearly two years. Out of my nature has come wild despair; an abandonment to grief that was piteous even to look at; terrible and impotent rage; bitterness and scorn; anguish that wept aloud; misery that could find no voice; sorrow that was dumb. I have passed through every possible mood of suffering. Better than Wordsworth himself I know what Wordsworth meant when he said—

> *Suffering is permanent, obscure, and dark*
> *And has the nature of infinity.*

But while there were times when I rejoiced in the idea that my sufferings were to be endless, I could not bear them to be without meaning. Now I find hidden somewhere away in my nature something that tells me that nothing in the whole world is meaningless, and suffering least of all. That something hidden away in my nature, like a treasure in a field, is Humility.

It is the last thing left in me, and the best: the ultimate discovery at which I have arrived, the starting-point for a fresh development. It has come to me right out of myself, so I know that it has come at the proper time. It could not have come before, nor later. Had anyone told me of it, I would have rejected it. Had it been brought to me, I would have refused it. As I found it, I want to keep it. I must do so. It is the one thing that has in it the elements of life, of a new life, *Vita Nuova* for me. Of all things it is the strangest. One cannot acquire it, except by surrendering everything that one has. It is only when one has lost all things, that one knows that one possesses it.

> *The first thing that I have got to do is to free myself from any possible bitterness of feeling against the world.*

Now I have realized that it is in me, I see quite clearly what I ought to do; in fact, must do. And when I use such a phrase as that, I need not say that I am not alluding to any external sanction or command. I admit none. I am far more of an individualist than I ever was. Nothing seems to me of the smallest value except what one gets out of oneself. My nature is seeking a fresh mode of self-realization. That is all I am concerned with. And the first thing that I have got to do is to free myself from any possible bitterness of feeling against the world.

I am completely penniless, and absolutely homeless. Yet there are worse things in the world than that. I am quite candid when I say that rather than go out from this prison with bitterness in my heart against the world, I would gladly and readily beg my bread from door to door. If I got nothing from the house of the rich I would get something at the house of the poor. Those who have much are often greedy; those who have little always share. I would not a bit mind sleeping in the cool grass in summer, and when winter came on sheltering myself by the warm close-thatched rick, or under the penthouse of a great barn, provided I had love in my heart. The external things of life seem to me now of no importance at all. You can see to what intensity of individualism I have arrived—or am arriving rather, for the journey is long, and 'where I walk there are thorns.'

> **When you really want love you will find it waiting for you.**

Of course I know that to ask alms on the highway is not to be my lot, and that if ever I lie in the cool grass at night-time it will be to write sonnets to the moon. When I go out of prison, Robbie will be waiting for me on the other side of the big iron-studded gate, and he is the symbol, not merely of his own affection, but of the affection of many others besides. I believe I am to have enough to live on for about eighteen months at any rate, so that if I may not write beautiful books, I may at least read beautiful books; and what joy can be greater? After that, I hope to be able to recreate my creative faculty.

But were things different: had I not a friend left in the world; were there not a single house open to me in pity; had I to accept the wallet and ragged cloak of sheer penury: as long as I am free from all resentment, hardness and scorn, I would be able to face life with much more calm and confidence than I would were my body in purple and fine linen, and the soul within me sick with hate.

And I really shall have no difficulty. When you really want love you will find it waiting for you.

I need not say that my task does not end there. It would be comparatively easy if it did. There is much more before me. I have hills far steeper to climb, valleys much darker to pass through. And I have to get it all out of myself.

NEITHER religion, morality, nor reason can help me at all.

Morality does not help me. I am a born antinomian. I am one of those who are made for exceptions, not for laws. But while I see that there is nothing wrong in what one does, I see that there is something wrong in what one becomes. It is well to have learned that.

Religion does not help me. The faith that others give to what is unseen, I give to what one can touch, and look at. My gods dwell in temples made with hands; and within the circle of actual experience is my creed made perfect and complete: too complete, it may be, for like many or all of those who have placed their heaven in this earth, I have found in it not merely the beauty of heaven, but the horror of hell also. When I think about religion at all, I feel as if I would like to found an order for those who *cannot* believe: the Confraternity of the Faithless, one might call it, where on an altar, on which no taper burned, a priest, in whose heart peace had no dwelling, might celebrate with unblessed bread and a chalice empty of wine. Every thing to be true must become a religion. And agnosticism should have its ritual no less than faith. It has sown its martyrs, it should reap its saints, and praise God daily for having hidden Himself from man. But whether it be faith or agnosticism, it must be nothing external to me. Its symbols must be of my own creating. Only that is spiritual which makes its own form. If I may not find its secret within myself, I shall never find it: if I have not got it already, it will never come to me.

Reason does not help me. It tells me that the laws under which I am convicted are wrong and unjust laws, and the system under which I have suffered a wrong and unjust system. But, somehow, I have got to make both of these things just and right to me. And exactly as in Art one is only concerned with what a particular thing is at a particular moment to oneself, so it is also in the ethical evolution of one's character. I have got to make everything that has happened to me good for me. The plank bed, the loathsome food, the hard ropes shredded into oakum till one's finger-tips grow dull with pain, the menial offices with which each day begins and finishes, the harsh orders that routine seems to necessitate, the dreadful dress that makes sorrow grotesque to look at, the silence, the solitude, the shame—each and all of these things I have to transform into a spiritual experience. There is not a

> The plank bed, the loathsome food, the hard ropes—each and all of these things I have to transform into a spiritual experience.

single degradation of the body which I must not try and make into a spiritualizing of the soul.

I want to get to the point when I shall be able to say quite simply, and without affectation, that the two great turning-points in my life were when my father sent me to Oxford, and when society sent me to prison. I will not say that prison is the best thing that could have happened to me: for that phrase would savor of too great bitterness towards myself. I would sooner say, or hear it said of me, that I was so typical a child of my age, that in my perversity, and for that perversity's sake, I turned the good things of my life to evil, and the evil things of my life to good.

What is said, however, by myself or by others, matters little. The important thing, the thing that lies before me, the thing that I have to do, if the brief remainder of my days is not to be maimed, marred, and incomplete, is to absorb into my nature all that has been done to me, to make it part of me, to accept it without complaint, fear, or reluctance. The supreme vice is shallowness. Whatever is realized is right.

When first I was put into prison some people advised me to try and forget who I was. It was ruinous advice. It is only by realizing what I am that I have found comfort of any kind. Now I am advised by others to try on my release to forget that I have ever been in a prison at all. I know that would be equally fatal. It would mean that I would always be haunted by an intolerable sense of disgrace, and that those things that are meant for me as much as for anybody else—the beauty of the sun and moon, the pageant of the seasons, the music of daybreak and the silence of great nights, the rain falling through the leaves, or the dew creeping over the grass and making it silver—would all be tainted for me, and lose their healing power, and their power of communicating joy. To regret one's own experiences is to arrest one's own development. To deny one's own experiences is to put a lie into the lips of one's own life. It is no less than a denial of the soul.

> To regret one's own experiences is to arrest one's own development.

For just as the body absorbs things of all kinds, things common and unclean no less than those that the priest or a vision has cleansed, and converts them into swiftness or strength, into the play of beautiful muscles and the moulding of fair flesh, into the curves and colors of the hair, the lips, the eye; so the soul in its turn has its nutritive functions also, and can transform into noble moods of thought and passions of high import what in itself is base, cruel and degrading; nay, more, may find in these its most august modes of assertion, and can often reveal itself most perfectly through what was intended to desecrate or destroy.

THE fact of my having been the common prisoner of a common gaol I must frankly accept, and, curious as it may seem, one of the things I shall have to teach myself is not to be ashamed of it. I must accept it as a punishment, and if one is ashamed of having been punished, one might just as well never have been punished at all. Of course there are many things of which I was convicted that I had not done, but then there are many things of which I was convicted that I had done, and a still greater number of things in my life for which I was never indicted at all. And as the gods are strange, and punish us for what is good and humane in us as much as for what is evil and perverse, I must accept the fact that one is punished for the good as well as for the evil that one does. I have no doubt that it is quite right one should be. It helps one, or should help one, to realize both, and not to be too conceited about either. And if I then am not ashamed of my punishment, as I hope not to be, I shall be able to think, and walk, and live with freedom.

Many men on their release carry their prison about with them into the air, and hide it as a secret disgrace in their hearts, and at length, like poor poisoned things, creep into some hole and die. It is wretched that they should have to do so, and it is wrong, terribly wrong, of society that it should force them to do so. Society takes upon itself the right to inflict appalling punishment on the individual, but it also has the supreme vice of shallowness, and fails to realize what it has done. When the man's punishment is over, it leaves him to himself; that is to say, it abandons him at the very moment when its highest duty towards him begins. It is really ashamed of its own actions, and shuns those whom it has punished, as people shun a creditor whose debt they cannot pay, or one on whom they have inflicted an irreparable, an irremediable wrong. I can claim on my side that if I realize what I have suffered, society should realize what it has inflicted on me; and that there should be no bitterness or hate on either side.

> *If I am not ashamed of my punishment, as I hope not to be, I shall be able to think, and walk, and live with freedom.*

Of course I know that from one point of view things will be made different for me than for others; must indeed, by the very nature of the case, be made so. The poor thieves and outcasts who are imprisoned here with me are in many respects more fortunate than I am. The little way in grey city or green field that saw their sin is small; to find those who know nothing of what they have done they need go no further than a bird might fly between the twilight and the dawn; but for me the world is shriveled to a handsbreadth, and everywhere I turn my name is written on the rocks in lead. For I have come, not from obscurity into the momentary notoriety of crime, but from a sort of eternity of fame to a sort of eternity of infamy, and sometimes seem to myself to have shown, if indeed it required showing, that between the famous and the infamous there is but one step, if as much as one.

> *If I can produce only one beautiful work of art I shall be able to rob malice of its venom, and cowardice of its sneer, and to pluck out the tongue of scorn by the roots.*

Still, in the very fact that people will recognize me wherever I go, and know all about my life, as far as its follies go, I can discern something good for me. It will force on me the necessity of again asserting myself as an artist, and as soon as I possibly can. If I can produce only one beautiful work of art I shall be able to rob malice of its venom, and cowardice of its sneer, and to pluck out the tongue of scorn by the roots.

And if life be, as it surely is, a problem to me, I am no less a problem to life. People must adopt some attitude towards me, and so pass judgment, both on themselves and me. I need not say I am not talking of particular individuals. The only people I would care to be with now are artists and people who have suffered: those who know what beauty is, and those who know what sorrow is: nobody else interests me. Nor am I making any demands on life. In all that I have said I am simply concerned with my own mental attitude towards life as a whole; and I feel that not to be ashamed of having been punished is one of the first points I must attain to, for the sake of my own perfection, and because I am so imperfect.

> *The only people I would care to be with now are artists and people who have suffered.*

THEN I must learn how to be happy. Once I knew it, or thought I knew it, by instinct. It was always springtime once in my heart. My temperament was akin to joy. I filled my life to the very brim with pleasure, as one might fill a cup to the very brim with wine. Now I am approaching life from a completely new standpoint, and even to conceive happiness is often extremely difficult for me. I remember during my first term at Oxford reading in Pater's *Renaissance*—that book which has had such strange influence over my life—how Dante places low in the Inferno those who willfully live in sadness; and going to the college library and turning to the passage in the *Divine Comedy* where beneath the dreary marsh lie those who were 'sullen in the sweet air,' saying for ever and ever through their sighs—

> *Tristi fummo*
> *Nell aer dolce che dal sol s'allegra.*

> [Sad were we,
> where the air was made sweet by the sun.]

I knew the church condemned *accidia* [apathy], but the whole idea seemed to me quite fantastic, just the sort of sin, I fancied, a priest who knew nothing about real life would invent. Nor could I understand how Dante, who says that 'sorrow remarries us to God,' could have been so harsh to those who were enamored of melancholy, if any such there really were. I had no idea that some day this would become to me one of the greatest temptations of my life.

While I was in Wandsworth prison I longed to die. It was my one desire. When after two months in the infirmary I was transferred here, and found myself growing gradually better in physical health, I was filled with rage. I determined to commit suicide on the very day on which I left prison. After a time that evil mood passed away, and I made up my mind to live, but to wear gloom as a king wears purple: never to smile again: to turn whatever house I entered into a house of mourning: to make my friends walk slowly in sadness with me: to teach them that melancholy is the true secret of life: to maim them with an alien sorrow: to mar them with my own pain. Now I feel quite differently. I see it would be both ungrateful and unkind of me to pull so long a face that when my friends came to see me they would have to make their faces still longer in order to show their sympathy; or, if I desired to entertain them, to invite them to sit down silently to bitter herbs and funeral baked meats. I must learn how to be cheerful and happy.

> *I long to live so that I can explore what is no less than a new world to me.*

The last two occasions on which I was allowed to see my friends here, I tried to be as cheerful as possible, and to show my cheerfulness, in order to make them some slight return for their trouble in coming all the way from town to see me. It is only a slight return, I know, but it is the one, I feel certain, that pleases them most. I saw Robbie for an hour on Saturday week, and I tried to give the fullest possible expression of the delight I really felt at our meeting. And that, in the views and ideas I am here shaping for myself, I am quite right is shown to me by the fact that now for the first time since my imprisonment I have a real desire for life.

> **Sorrow, and all that it teaches one, is my new world.**

There is before me so much to do, that I would regard it as a terrible tragedy if I died before I was allowed to complete at any rate a little of it. I see new developments in art and life, each one of which is a fresh mode of perfection. I long to live so that I can explore what is no less than a new world to me. Do you want to know what this new world is? I think you can guess what it is. It is the world in which I have been living. Sorrow, then, and all that it teaches one, is my new world.

I used to live entirely for pleasure. I shunned suffering and sorrow of every kind. I hated both. I resolved to ignore them as far as possible: to treat them, that is to say, as modes of imperfection. They were not part of my scheme of life. They had no place in my philosophy. My mother, who knew life as a whole, used often to quote to me Goethe's lines—written by Carlyle in a book he had given her years ago, and translated by him, I fancy, also:

> *Who never ate his bread in sorrow,*
> *Who never spent the midnight hours*
> *Weeping and waiting for the morrow—*
> *He knows you not, ye heavenly powers.*

They were the lines which that noble Queen of Prussia, whom Napoleon treated with such coarse brutality, used to quote in her humiliation and exile; they were the lines my mother often quoted in the troubles of her later life. I absolutely declined to accept or admit the enormous truth hidden in them. I could not understand it. I remember quite well how I used to tell her that I did not want to eat my bread in sorrow, or to pass any night weeping and watching for a more bitter dawn.

I had no idea that it was one of the special things that the Fates had in store for me: that for a whole year of my life, indeed, I was to do little else. But so has my portion been meted out to me; and during the last few months I have, after terrible difficulties and struggles, been able to comprehend some of the lessons hidden in the heart of pain. Clergymen and people who use phrases without wisdom sometimes talk of suffering as a mystery. It is really a revelation. One discerns things one never discerned before. One approaches the whole of history from a different standpoint. What one had felt dimly, through instinct, about art, is intellectually and emotionally realized with perfect clearness of vision and absolute intensity of apprehension.

> *Sorrow, being the supreme emotion of which man is capable, is at once the type and test of all great art.*

I now see that sorrow, being the supreme emotion of which man is capable, is at once the type and test of all great art. What the artist is always looking for is the mode of existence in which soul and body are one and indivisible: in which the outward is expressive of the inward: in which form reveals. Of such modes of existence there are not a few: youth and the arts preoccupied with youth may serve as a model for us at one moment: at another we may like to think that, in its subtlety and sensitiveness of impression, its suggestion of a spirit dwelling in external things and making its raiment of earth and air, of mist and city alike, and in its morbid sympathy of its moods, and tones, and colors, modern landscape art is realizing for us pictorially what was realized in such plastic perfection by the Greeks. Music, in which all subject is absorbed in expression and cannot be separated from it, is a complex example, and a flower or a child a simple example, of what I mean; but sorrow is the ultimate type both in life and art.

> *Out of sorrow have the worlds been built, and at the birth of a child or a star there is pain.*

Behind joy and laughter there may be a temperament, coarse, hard and callous. But behind sorrow there is always sorrow. Pain, unlike pleasure, wears no mask. Truth in art is not any correspondence between the essential idea and the accidental existence; it is not the resemblance of shape to shadow, or of the form mirrored in the crystal to the form itself; it is no echo coming from a hollow hill, any more than it is a silver well of water in the valley that shows the moon to the moon and Narcissus to Narcissus. Truth in art is the unity of a thing with itself: the outward rendered expressive of the inward: the soul made incarnate: the body instinct with spirit. For this reason there is no truth comparable to sorrow. There are times when sorrow seems to me to be the only truth. Other things may be illusions of the eye or the appetite, made to blind the one and cloy the other, but out of sorrow have the worlds been built, and at the birth of a child or a star there is pain.

> *The secret of life is suffering. It is what is hidden behind everything.*

More than this, there is about sorrow an intense, an extraordinary reality. I have said of myself that I was one who stood in symbolic relations to the art and culture of my age. There is not a single wretched man in this wretched place along with me who does not stand in symbolic relation to the very secret of life. For the secret of life is suffering. It is what is hidden behind everything. When we begin to live, what is sweet is so sweet to us, and what is bitter so bitter, that we inevitably direct all our desires towards pleasures, and seek not merely for a 'month or twain to feed on honeycomb,' but for all our years to taste no other food, ignorant all the while that we may really be starving the soul.

I remember talking once on this subject to one of the most beautiful personalities I have ever known: a woman, whose sympathy and noble kindness to me, both before and since the tragedy of my imprisonment, have been beyond power and description; one who has really assisted me, though she does not know it, to bear the burden of my troubles more than anyone else in the whole world has, and all through the mere fact of her existence, through her being what she is—partly an ideal and partly an influence: a suggestion of what one might become as well as a real help towards becoming it; a soul that renders the common air sweet, and makes what is spiritual seem as simple and natural as sunlight or the sea: one for whom beauty and sorrow walk hand in hand, and have the same message.

On the occasion of which I am thinking I recall distinctly how I said to her that there was enough suffering in one narrow London lane to show that God did not love man, and that wherever there was any sorrow, though but that of a child, in some little garden weeping over a fault that it had or had not committed, the whole face of creation was completely marred. I was entirely wrong. She told me so, but I could not believe her. I was not in the sphere in which such belief was to be attained to.

Now it seems to me that love of some kind is the only possible explanation of the extraordinary amount of suffering that there is in the world. I cannot conceive of any other explanation. I am convinced that there is no other, and that if the world has indeed, as I have said, been built of sorrow, it has been built by the hands of love, because in no other way could the soul of man, for whom the world was made, reach the full stature of its perfection. Pleasure for the beautiful body, but pain for the beautiful soul.

WHEN I say that I am convinced of these things, I speak with too much pride. Far off, like a perfect pearl, one can see the city of God. It is so wonderful that it seems as if a child could reach it in a summer's day. And so a child could. But with me and such as me it is different. One can realize a thing in a single moment, but one loses it in the long hours that follow with leaden feet. It is so difficult to keep 'heights that the soul is competent to gain.' We think in eternity, but we move slowly through time; and how slowly time goes with us who lie in prison I need not tell again, nor of the weariness and despair that creep back into one's cell, and into the cell of one's heart, with such strange insistence that one has, as it were, to garnish and sweep one's house for their coming, as for an unwelcome guest, or a bitter master, or a slave whose slave it is one's chance or choice to be.

And, though at present my friends may find it a hard thing to believe, it is true none the less, that for them living in freedom and idleness and comfort it is more easy to learn the lessons of humility than it is for me, who begin the day by going down on my knees and washing the floor of my cell. For prison life with its endless privations and restrictions makes one rebellious. The most terrible thing about it is not that it breaks one's heart—hearts are made to be broken—but that it turns one's heart to stone. One sometimes feels that it is only with a front of brass and a lip of scorn that one can get through the day at all. And he who is in a state of rebellion cannot receive grace, to use the phrase of which the Church is so fond—so rightly fond, I dare say—for

> *It seems to me that love of some kind is the only possible explanation of the extraordinary amount of suffering that there is in the world.*

in life as in art the mood of rebellion closes up the channels of the soul, and shuts out the airs of heaven. Yet I must learn these lessons here, if I am to learn them anywhere, and must be filled with joy if my feet are on the right road and my face set towards 'the gate which is called beautiful,' though I may fall many times in the mire and often in the mist go astray.

THIS 'new life,' as through my love of Dante I like sometimes to call it, is of course no new life at all, but simply the continuance, by means of development, and evolution, of my former life. I remember when I was at Oxford saying to one of my friends as we were strolling round Magdalen's narrow bird-haunted walks one morning in the year before I took my degree, that I wanted to eat of the fruit of all the trees in the garden of the world, and that I was going out into the world with that passion in my soul. And so, indeed, I went out, and so I lived. My only mistake was that I confined myself so exclusively to the trees of what seemed to me the sunlit side of the garden, and shunned the other side for its shadow and its gloom. Failure, disgrace, poverty, sorrow, despair, suffering, tears even, the broken words that come from lips in pain, remorse that makes one walk on thorns, conscience that condemns, self-abasement that punishes, the misery that puts ashes on its head, the anguish that chooses sack-cloth for its raiment and into its own drink puts gall:—all these were things of which I was afraid. And as I had determined to know nothing of them, I was forced to taste each of them in turn, to feed on them, to have for a season, indeed, no other food at all.

I don't regret for a single moment having lived for pleasure. I did it to the full, as one should do everything that one does. There was no pleasure I did not experience. I threw the pearl of my soul into a cup of wine. I went down the primrose path to the sound of flutes. I lived on honeycomb. But to have continued the same life would have been wrong because it would have been limiting. I had to pass on. The other half of the garden had its secrets for me also.

> *I don't regret for a single moment having lived for pleasure. I did it to the full, as one should do everything that one does.*

Of course all this is foreshadowed and prefigured in my books. Some of it is in *The Happy Prince*, some of it in *The Young King*, notably in the passage where the bishop says to the kneeling boy, 'Is not He who made misery wiser than thou art?' a phrase which when I wrote it seemed to me little more than a phrase; a great deal of it is hidden away in the note of doom that like a purple thread runs through the texture of *Dorian Gray*; in *The Critic as Artist* it is set forth in many colors; in *The Soul of Man* it is written down, and in letters too easy to read; it is one of the refrains whose recurring motifs make *Salome* so like a piece of music and bind it together as a ballad; in the prose poem of the man who from the bronze of the image of the 'Pleasure that liveth for a moment' has to make the image of the 'Sorrow that abideth for ever' it is incarnate. It could not have been otherwise. At every single moment of one's life one is what one is going to be no less than what one has been. Art is a symbol, because man is a symbol.

> *The artistic life is simply self-development.*

It is, if I can fully attain to it, the ultimate realization of the artistic life. For the artistic life is simply self-development. Humility in the artist is his frank acceptance of all experiences, just as love in the artist is simply the sense of beauty that reveals to the world its body and its soul. In *Marius the Epicurean* Pater seeks to reconcile the artistic life with the life of religion, in the deep, sweet, and austere sense of the word. But Marius is little more than a spectator: an ideal spectator indeed, and one to whom it is given 'to contemplate the spectacle of life with appropriate emotions,' which Wordsworth defines as the poet's true aim; yet a spectator merely, and perhaps a little too much occupied with the comeliness of the benches of the sanctuary to notice that it is the sanctuary of sorrow that he is gazing at.

I see a far more intimate and immediate connection between the true life of Christ and the true life of the artist; and I take a keen pleasure in the reflection that long before sorrow had made my days her own and bound me to her wheel I had written in *The Soul of Man* that he who would lead a Christ-like life must be entirely and absolutely himself, and had taken as my types not merely the shepherd on the hillside and the prisoner in his cell, but also the painter to whom the world is a pageant and the poet for whom the world is a song. I remember saying once to André Gide, as we sat together in some Paris café, that while metaphysics had but little real interest for me, and morality absolutely none, there was nothing that either Plato or Christ had said that could not be transferred immediately into the sphere of Art and there find its complete fulfillment.

*He is despised and rejected of men;
a man of sorrows, and acquainted with grief.*
—Isaiah 53:3

Nor is it merely that we can discern in Christ that close union of personality with perfection which forms the real distinction between the classical and romantic movement in life, but the very basis of his nature was the same as that of the nature of the artist—an intense and flamelike imagination. He realized in the entire sphere of human relations that imaginative sympathy which in the sphere of Art is the sole secret of creation. He understood the leprosy of the leper, the darkness of the blind, the fierce misery of those who live for pleasure, the strange poverty of the rich.

Some one wrote to me in trouble, 'When you are not on your pedestal you are not interesting.' How remote was the writer from what Matthew Arnold calls 'the Secret of Jesus.' Either would have taught him that whatever happens to another happens to oneself, and if you want an inscription to read at dawn and at night-time, and for pleasure or for pain, write up on the walls of your house in letters for the sun to gild and the moon to silver, 'Whatever happens to oneself happens to another.'

CHRIST'S place indeed is with the poets. His whole conception of humanity sprang right out of the imagination and can only be realized by it. What God was to the pantheist, man was to Him. He was the first to conceive the divided races as a unity. Before his time there had been gods and men, and, feeling through the mysticism of sympathy that in himself each had been made incarnate, he calls himself the Son of the one or the Son of the other, according to his mood. More than anyone else in history he wakes in us that temper of wonder to which romance always appeals.

> *The very basis of Christ's nature was the same as that of the nature of the artist— an intense and flamelike imagination.*

There is still something to me almost incredible in the idea of a young Galilean peasant imagining that he could bear on his own shoulders the burden of the entire world; all that had already been done and suffered, and all that was yet to be done and suffered: the sins of Nero, of Caesar Borgia, of Alexander VI, and of him who was Emperor of Rome and Priest of the Sun: the sufferings of those whose names are legion and whose dwelling is among the tombs: oppressed nationalities, factory children, thieves, people in prison, outcasts, those who are dumb under oppression and whose silence is heard only of God; and not merely imagining this but actually achieving it, so that at the present moment all who come in contact with his personality, even though they may neither bow to his altar nor kneel before his priest, in some way find that the ugliness of their sin is taken away and the beauty of their sorrow revealed to them.

I said of Christ that he ranks with the poets. That is true. Shelley and Sophocles are of his company. But his entire life also is the most wonderful of poems. For 'pity and terror' there is nothing in the entire cycle of Greek tragedy to touch it. The absolute purity of the protagonist raises the entire scheme to a height of romantic art from which the sufferings of Thebes and Pelops' line are by their very horror excluded, and shows how wrong Aristotle was when he said in his treatise on the drama that it would be impossible to bear the spectacle of one blameless in pain. Nor in Aeschylus nor Dante, those stern masters of tenderness, in Shakespeare, the most purely human of all the great artists, in the whole of Celtic myth and legend, where the loveliness of the world is shown through a mist of tears, and the life of a man is no more than the life of a

> *More than anyone else in history he wakes in us that temper of wonder to which romance always appeals.*

flower, is there anything that, for sheer simplicity of pathos wedded and made one with sublimity of tragic effect, can be said to equal or even approach the last act of Christ's passion. The supper with his companions, one of whom has already sold him for a price; the anguish in the quiet moonlit garden; the false friend coming close to him so as to betray him with a kiss; the friend who still believed in him, and on whom as on a rock he had hoped to build a house of refuge for Man, denying him as the bird cried to the dawn; his own utter loneliness, his submission, his acceptance of everything; and along with it all such scenes as the high priest of orthodoxy rending his raiment in wrath, and the magistrate of civil justice calling for water in the vain hope of cleansing himself of that stain of innocent blood that makes him the scarlet figure of history; the coronation ceremony of sorrow, one of the most wonderful things in the whole of recorded time; the crucifixion of the Innocent One before the eyes of his mother and of the disciple whom he loved; the soldiers gambling and throwing dice for his clothes; the terrible death by which he gave the world its most eternal symbol; and his final burial in the tomb of the rich man, his body swathed in Egyptian linen with costly spices and perfumes as though he had been a king's son.

When one contemplates all this from the point of view of art alone one cannot but be grateful that the supreme office of the Church should be the playing of the tragedy without the shedding of blood: the mystical presentation, by means of dialogue and costume and gesture even, of the Passion of her Lord; and it is always a source of pleasure and awe to me to remember that the ultimate survival of the Greek chorus, lost elsewhere to art, is to be found in the servitor answering the priest at Mass.

> *Christ saw that love was the first secret of the world for which the wise men had been looking.*

Yet the whole life of Christ—so entirely may sorrow and beauty be made one in their meaning and manifestation—is really an idyll, though it ends with the veil of the temple being rent, and the darkness coming over the face of the earth, and the stone rolled to the door of the sepulcher. One always thinks of him as a young bridegroom with his companions, as indeed he somewhere describes himself; as a shepherd straying through a valley with his sheep in search of green meadow or cool stream; as a singer trying to build out of the music the walls of the City of God; or as a lover for whose love the whole world was too small. His miracles seem to me to be as exquisite as the coming of spring, and quite as natural. I see no difficulty at all in believing that such was the charm of his personality that his mere presence could bring peace to souls in anguish, and that those who touched his garments or his hands forgot their pain; or that as he passed by on the highway of life people who had seen nothing of life's mystery, saw it clearly, and others who had been deaf to every voice but that of pleasure heard for the first time the voice of love and found it as 'musical as Apollo's lute'; or that evil passions fled at his approach, and men whose dull unimaginative lives had been but a mode of death rose as it were from the grave when he called them; or that when he taught on the hillside the multitude forgot their hunger and thirst and the cares of this world, and that to his friends who listened to him as he sat at meat the coarse food seemed delicate, and the water had the taste of good wine, and the whole house became full of the odor and sweetness of nard.

> *Above all, Christ is the most supreme of individualists.*

Renan in his *Vie de Jesus*—that gracious fifth gospel, the gospel according to St. Thomas, one might call it—says somewhere that Christ's great achievement was that he made himself as much loved after his death as he had been during his lifetime. And certainly, if his place is among the poets, he is the leader of all the lovers. He saw that love was the first secret of the world for which the wise men had been looking, and that it was only through love that one could approach either the heart of the leper or the feet of God.

Above all, Christ is the most supreme of individualists. Humility, like the artistic, acceptance of all experiences, is merely a mode of manifestation. It is man's soul that Christ is always looking for. He calls it 'God's Kingdom,' and finds it in everyone. He compares it to little things, to a tiny seed, to a handful of leaven, to a pearl. That is because one realizes one's soul only by getting rid of all alien passions, all acquired culture, and all external possessions, be they good or evil.

> *He calls [the soul] 'God's Kingdom,' and finds it in everyone.*

I bore up against everything with some stubbornness of will and much rebellion of nature, till I had absolutely nothing left in the world but one thing. I had lost my name, my position, my happiness, my freedom, my wealth. I was a prisoner and a pauper. But I still had my children left. Suddenly they were taken away from me by the law. It was a blow so appalling that I did not know what to do, so I flung myself on my knees, and bowed my head, and wept, and said, 'The body of a child is as the body of the Lord: I am not worthy of either.' That moment seemed to save me. I saw then that the only thing for me was to accept everything.

Since then—curious as it will no doubt sound—I have been happier. It was of course my soul in its ultimate essence that I had reached. In many ways I had been its enemy, but I found it waiting for me as a friend. When one comes in contact with the soul it makes one simple as a child, as Christ said one should be.

> *It is tragic how few people ever 'possess their souls' before they die.*

It is tragic how few people ever 'possess their souls' before they die. 'Nothing is more rare in any man,' says Emerson, 'than an act of his own.' It is quite true. Most people are other people. Their thoughts are some one else's opinions, their lives a mimicry, their passions a quotation. Christ was not merely the supreme individualist, but he was the first individualist in history. People have tried to make him out an ordinary philanthropist, or ranked him as an altruist with the scientific and sentimental. But he was really neither one nor the other.

Pity he has, of course, for the poor, for those who are shut up in prisons, for the lowly, for the wretched; but he has far more pity for the rich, for the hard hedonists, for those who waste their freedom in becoming slaves to things, for those who wear soft raiment and live in kings' houses. Riches and pleasure seemed to him to be really greater tragedies than poverty or sorrow. And as for altruism, who knew better than he that it is vocation not volition that determines us, and that one cannot gather grapes of thorns or figs from thistles?

To live for others as a definite self-conscious aim was not his creed. It was not the basis of his creed. When he says, 'Forgive your enemies,' it is not for the sake of the enemy, but for one's own sake that he says so, and because love is more beautiful than hate. In his own entreaty to the young man, 'Sell all that thou hast and give to the poor,' it is not of the state of the poor that he is thinking but of the soul of the young man, the soul that wealth was marring. In his view of life he is one with the artist who knows that by the inevitable law of self-perfection, the poet must sing, and the sculptor think in bronze, and the painter make the world a mirror for his moods, as surely and as certainly as the hawthorn must blossom in spring, and the corn turn to gold at harvest-time, and the moon in her ordered wanderings change from shield to sickle, and from sickle to shield.

But while Christ did not say to men, 'Live for others,' he pointed out that there was no difference at all between the lives of others and one's own life. By this means he gave to man an extended, a Titan personality. Since his coming the history of each separate individual is, or can be made, the history of the world. Of course, culture has intensified the personality of man. Art has made us myriad-minded. Those who have the artistic temperament go into exile with Dante and learn how salt is the bread of others, and how steep their stairs; they catch for a moment the serenity and calm of Goethe, and yet know but too well that Baudelaire cried to God—

> *O Seigneur, donnez moi la force et le courage*
> *De contempler mon corps et mon coeur sans dégoût.*

> *[O Lord, give me strength and courage*
> *To contemplate my body and my heart without disgust.]*

Out of Shakespeare's sonnets they draw, to their own hurt it may be, the secret of his love and make it their own; they look with new eyes on modern life, because they have listened to one of Chopin's nocturnes, or handled Greek things, or read the story of the passion of some dead man for some dead woman whose hair was like threads of fine gold, and whose mouth was as a pomegranate. But the sympathy of the artistic temperament is necessarily with what has found expression. In words or in colors, in music or in marble, behind the painted masks of an Aeschylean play, or through some Sicilian shepherds' pierced and jointed reeds, the man and his message must have been revealed.

> *While Christ did not say to men, 'Live for others,' he pointed out that there was no difference at all between the lives of others and one's own life.*

To the artist, expression is the only mode under which he can conceive life at all. To him what is dumb is dead. But to Christ it was not so. With a width and wonder of imagination that fills one almost with awe, he took the entire world of the inarticulate, the voiceless world of pain, as his kingdom, and made of himself its eternal mouthpiece. Those of whom I have spoken, who are dumb under oppression, and 'whose silence is heard only of God,' he chose as his brothers. He sought to become eyes to the blind, ears to the deaf, and a cry in the lips of those whose tongues had been tied. His desire was to be to the myriads who had found no utterance a very trumpet through which they might call to heaven. And feeling, with the artistic nature of one to whom suffering and sorrow were modes through which he could realize his conception of the beautiful, that an idea is of no value till it becomes incarnate and is made an image, he made of himself the image of the Man of Sorrows, and as such has fascinated and dominated art as no Greek god ever succeeded in doing.

> *He sought to become eyes to the blind, ears to the deaf, and a cry in the lips of those whose tongues had been tied.*

For the Greek gods, in spite of the white and red of their fair fleet limbs, were not really what they appeared to be. The curved brow of Apollo was like the sun's disc crescent over a hill at dawn, and his feet were as the wings of the morning, but he himself had been cruel to Marsyas and had made Niobe childless. In the steel shields of Athena's eyes there had been no pity for Arachne; the pomp and peacocks of Hera were all that was really noble about her; and the Father of the Gods himself had been too fond of the daughters of men. The two most deeply suggestive figures of Greek Mythology were, for religion, Demeter, an Earth Goddess, not one of the Olympians, and for art, Dionysus, the son of a mortal woman to whom the moment of his birth had proved also the moment of her death.

But Life itself from its lowliest and most humble sphere produced one far more marvelous than the mother of Proserpina or the son of Semele. Out of the Carpenter's shop at Nazareth had come a personality infinitely greater than any made by myth and legend, and one, strangely enough, destined to reveal to the world the mystical meaning of wine and the real beauties of the lilies of the field as none, either on Cithaeron or at Enna, had ever done.

> *He made of himself the image of the Man of Sorrows, and as such has fascinated and dominated art as no Greek god ever succeeded in doing.*

THE song of Isaiah, 'He is despised and rejected of men; a man of sorrows, and acquainted with grief; and we hid as it were our faces from him; he was despised, and we esteemed him not,' had seemed to him to prefigure himself, and in him the prophecy was fulfilled.

We must not be afraid of such a phrase. Every single work of art is the fulfillment of a prophecy: for every work of art is the conversion of an idea into an image. Every single human being should be the fulfillment of a prophecy: for every human being should be the realization of some ideal, either in the mind of God or in the mind of man. Christ found the type and fixed it, and the dream of a Virgilian poet, either at Jerusalem or at Babylon, became in the long progress of the centuries incarnate in him for whom the world was waiting.

To me one of the things in history the most to be regretted is that the Christ's own renaissance, which has produced the Cathedral at Chartres, the Arthurian cycle of legends, the life of St. Francis of Assisi, the art of Giotto, and Dante's *Divine Comedy*, was not allowed to develop on its own lines, but was interrupted and spoiled by the dreary classical Renaissance that gave us Petrarch, and Raphael's frescoes, and Palladian architecture, and formal French tragedy, and St. Paul's Cathedral, and Pope's poetry, and everything that is made from without and by dead rules, and does not spring from within through some spirit informing it. But wherever there is a romantic movement in art there somehow, and under some form, is Christ, or the soul of Christ. He is in *Romeo and Juliet*, in the *Winter's Tale*, in

Provençal poetry, in the *Ancient Mariner*, in *La Belle Dame sans merci*, and in Chatterton's *Ballad of Charity*.

We owe to him the most diverse things and people. Hugo's *Les Misérables*, Baudelaire's *Fleurs du Mal*, the note of pity in Russian novels, Verlaine and Verlaine's poems, the stained glass and tapestries and the quattrocento work of Burne-Jones and Morris, belong to him no less than the tower of Giotto, Lancelot and Guinevere, Tannhäuser, the troubled romantic marbles of Michelangelo, pointed architecture, and the love of children and flowers—for both of which, indeed, in classical art there was but little place, hardly enough for them to grow or play in, but which, from the twelfth century down to our own day, have been continually making their appearances in art, under various modes and at various times, coming fitfully and willfully, as children, as flowers, are apt to do: spring always seeming to one as if the flowers had been in hiding, and only came out into the sun because they were afraid that grown up people would grow tired of looking for them and give up the search; and the life of a

> *Every single work of art is the fulfillment of a prophecy: for every work of art is the conversion of an idea into an image.*

child being no more than an April day on which there is both rain and sun for the narcissus.

It is the imaginative quality of Christ's own nature that makes him this palpitating centre of romance. The strange figures of poetic drama and ballad are made by the imagination of others, but out of his own imagination entirely did Jesus of Nazareth create himself. The cry of Isaiah had really no more to do with his coming than the song of the nightingale has to do with the rising of the moon—no more, though perhaps no less. He was the denial as well as the affirmation of prophecy. For every expectation that he fulfilled there was another that he destroyed. 'In all beauty,' says Bacon, 'there is some strangeness of proportion,' and of those who are born of the spirit—of those, that is to say, who like himself are dynamic forces—Christ says that they are like the wind that 'bloweth where it listeth, and no man can tell whence it cometh and whither it goeth.' That is why he is so fascinating to artists. He has all the color elements of life: mystery, strangeness, pathos, suggestion, ecstasy, love. He appeals to the temper of wonder,

> *Christ has all the color elements of life: mystery, strangeness, pathos, suggestion, ecstasy, love.*

and creates that mood in which alone he can be understood.

And to me it is a joy to remember that if he is 'of imagination all compact,' the world itself is of the same substance. I said in *Dorian Gray* that the great sins of the world take place in the brain: but it is in the brain that everything takes place. We know now that we do not see with the eyes or hear with the ears. They are really channels for the transmission, adequate or inadequate, of sense impressions. It is in the brain that the poppy is red, that the apple is odorous, that the skylark sings.

> *He appeals to the temper of wonder, and creates that mood in which alone he can be understood.*

Of late I have been studying with diligence the four prose poems about Christ. At Christmas I managed to get hold of a Greek Testament, and every morning, after I had cleaned my cell and polished my tins, I read a little of the Gospels, a dozen verses taken by chance anywhere. It is a delightful way of opening the day. Everyone, even in a turbulent, ill-disciplined life, should do the same. Endless repetition, in and out of season, has spoiled for us the freshness, the naïveté, the simple romantic charm of the Gospels. We hear them read far too often and far too badly, and all repetition is anti-spiritual. When one returns to the Greek; it is like going into a garden of lilies out of some, narrow and dark house.

And to me, the pleasure is doubled by the reflection that it is extremely probable that we have the actual terms, the *ipsissima verba*, used by Christ. It was always supposed that Christ talked in Aramaic. Even Renan thought so. But now we know that the Galilean peasants, like the Irish peasants of our own day, were bilingual, and that Greek was the ordinary language of intercourse all over Palestine, as indeed all over the Eastern world. I never liked the idea that we knew of Christ's own words only through a translation of a translation. It is a delight to me to think that as far as his conversation was concerned, Charmides might have listened to him, and Socrates reasoned with him, and Plato understood him: that he really said εγω ειμι ο ποιμην ο καλος ['I am the good shepherd'], that when he thought of the lilies of the field and how they neither toil nor spin, his absolute expression was καταγαθετε τα κρίνα του αγρου τως αυξανει ου κοπιυ ουδε νηθει, and that his last word when he cried out 'my life has been completed, has reached its fulfillment, has been perfected,' was exactly as St. John tells us it was: τετέλεσται—no more.

While in reading the Gospels—particularly that of St. John himself, or whatever early Gnostic took his name and mantle—I see the continual assertion of the imagination as the basis of all spiritual and material life, I see also that to Christ imagination was simply a form of love, and that to him love was lord in the fullest meaning of the phrase. Some six weeks ago I was allowed by the doctor to have white bread to eat instead of the coarse black or brown bread of ordinary prison fare. It is a great delicacy. It will sound strange that dry bread could possibly be a delicacy to anyone. To me it is so much so that at the close of each meal I carefully eat whatever crumbs may be left on my tin plate, or have fallen on the rough towel that one uses as a cloth so as not to soil one's table; and I do so not from hunger—I get now quite sufficient food—but simply in order that nothing should be wasted of what is given to me. So one should look on love.

Christ, like all fascinating personalities, had the power of not merely saying beautiful things himself, but

> *Most people live for love and admiration. But it is by love and admiration that we should live.*

of making other people say beautiful things to him; and I love the story St. Mark tells us about the Greek woman, who, when as a trial of her faith he said to her that he could not give her the bread of the children of Israel, answered him that the little dogs—(κυναρια, 'little dogs' it should be rendered)—who are under the table eat of the crumbs that the children let fall. Most people live for love and admiration. But it is by love and admiration that we should live. If any love is shown us we should recognize that we are quite unworthy of it. Nobody is worthy to be loved. The fact that God loves man shows us that in the divine order of ideal things it is written that eternal love is to be given to what is eternally unworthy. Or if that phrase seems to be a bitter one to bear, let us say that everyone is worthy of love, except him who thinks that he is. Love is a sacrament that should be taken kneeling, and *Domine, non sum dignus* [Lord, I am not worthy] should be on the lips and in the hearts of those who receive it.

> *Love is a sacrament that should be taken kneeling.*

If ever I write again, in the sense of producing artistic work, there are just two subjects on which and through which I desire to express myself: one is 'Christ as the precursor of the romantic movement in life': the other is 'The artistic life considered in its relation to conduct.' The first is, of course, intensely fascinating, for I see in Christ not merely the essentials of the supreme romantic type, but all the accidents, the willfulness even, of the romantic temperament also. He was the first person who ever said to people that they should live 'flower-like lives.' He fixed the phrase. He took children as the type of what people should try to become. He held them up as examples to their elders, which I myself have always thought the chief use of children, if what is perfect should have a use. Dante describes the soul of a man as coming from the hand of God 'weeping and laughing like a little child,' and Christ also saw that the soul of each one should be *a guisa di fanciulla che piangendo e ridendo pargoleggia*. He felt that life was changeful, fluid, active, and that to allow it to be stereotyped into any form was death. He saw that people should not be too serious over material, common interests: that to be unpractical was to be a great thing: that one should not bother too much over affairs. The birds didn't, why should man? He is charming when he says, 'Take no thought for the morrow; is not the soul more than meat? is not the body more than raiment?' A Greek might have used the latter phrase. It is full of Greek feeling. But only Christ could have said both, and so summed up life perfectly for us.

His morality is all sympathy, just what morality should be. If the only thing that he ever said had been, 'Her sins are forgiven her because she loved much,' it would have been worth while dying to have said it. His justice is all poetical justice, exactly what justice should be. The beggar goes to heaven because he has been unhappy. I cannot conceive a better reason for his being sent there. The people who work for an hour in the vineyard in the cool of the evening receive just as much reward as those who have toiled there all day long in the hot sun. Why shouldn't they? Probably no one deserved anything. Or perhaps they were a different kind of people. Christ had no patience with the dull lifeless mechanical systems that treat people as if they were things, and so treat everybody alike: for him there were no laws: there were exceptions merely,

> *He was the first person who ever said to people that they should live 'flower-like lives.'*

as if anybody, or anything, for that matter, was like aught else in the world!

That which is the very keynote of romantic art was to him the proper basis of natural life. He saw no other basis. And when they brought him one, taken in the very act of sin and showed him her sentence written in the law, and asked him what was to be done, he wrote with his finger on the ground as though he did not hear them, and finally, when they pressed him again, looked up and said, 'Let him of you who has never sinned be the first to throw the stone at her.' It was worth while living to have said that.

> *Christ had no patience with the dull lifeless mechanical systems that treat people as if they were things.*

LIKE all poetical natures he loved ignorant people. He knew that in the soul of one who is ignorant there is always room for a great idea. But he could not stand stupid people, especially those who are made stupid by education: people who are full of opinions not one of which they even understand, a peculiarly modern type, summed up by Christ when he describes it as the type of one who has the key of knowledge, cannot use it himself, and does not allow other people to use it, though it may be made to open the gate of God's Kingdom.

His chief war was against the Philistines. That is the war every child of light has to wage. Philistinism was the note of the age and community in which he lived. In their heavy inaccessibility to ideas, their dull respectability, their tedious orthodoxy, their worship of vulgar success, their entire preoccupation with the gross materialistic side of life, and their ridiculous estimate of themselves and their importance, the respected people of Jerusalem in Christ's day were the exact counterparts of the British Philistines of our own.

Christ mocked at the 'whited sepulcher' of respectability, and fixed that phrase for ever. He treated worldly success as a thing absolutely to be despised. He saw nothing in it at all. He looked on wealth as an encumbrance to a man. He would not hear of life being sacrificed to any system of thought or morals. He pointed out that forms and ceremonies were made for man, not man for forms and ceremonies. He took sabbatarianism as a type of the things that should be set at nought. The cold philanthropies, the ostentatious public charities, the tedious formalisms so dear to the middle-class mind, he exposed with utter and relentless scorn. To us, what is termed orthodoxy is merely a facile unintelligent acquiescence; but to them, and in their hands, it was a terrible and paralyzing tyranny. Christ swept it aside. He showed that the spirit alone was of value. He took a keen pleasure in pointing out to them that though they were always reading the law and the prophets, they had not really the smallest idea of what either of them meant. In opposition to their tithing of each separate day into the fixed routine of prescribed duties, as they tithe mint and rue, he preached the enormous importance of living completely for the moment.

> *He would not hear of life being sacrificed to any system of thought or morals.*

Those whom he saved from their sins are saved simply for beautiful moments in their lives. Mary Magdalen, when she sees Christ, breaks the rich vase of alabaster that one of her seven lovers had given her, and spills the odorous spices over his tired dusty feet, and for that one moment's sake sits for ever with Ruth and Beatrice in the tresses of the snow-white rose of Paradise. All that Christ says to us by the way of a little warning is that every moment should be beautiful, that the soul should always be ready for the coming of the bridegroom, always waiting for the voice of the lover,

Philistinism being simply that side of man's nature that is not illumined by the imagination. He sees all the lovely influences of life as modes of light: the imagination itself is the world of light. The world is made by it, and yet the world cannot understand it: that is because the imagination is simply a manifestation of love, and it is love and the capacity for it that distinguishes one human being from another.

It is when he deals with a sinner that Christ is most romantic, in the sense of most real. The world had always loved the saint as being the nearest possible approach to the perfection of God. Christ, through some divine instinct in him, seems to have always loved the sinner as being the nearest possible approach to the perfection of man. His primary desire was not to reform people, any more than his primary desire was to a relieve suffering. To turn an interesting thief into a tedious honest man was not his aim. He would have thought little of the Prisoners' Aid Society and other modern movements of the kind. The conversion of a publican into a Pharisee would not have

> *Those whom he saved from their sins are saved simply for beautiful moments in their lives.*

seemed to him a great achievement. But in a manner not yet understood of the world he regarded sin and suffering as being in themselves beautiful holy things and modes of perfection.

It seems a very dangerous idea. It is—all great ideas are dangerous. That it was Christ's creed admits of no doubt. That it is the true creed I don't doubt myself.

Of course the sinner must repent. But why? Simply because otherwise he would be unable to realize what he had done. The moment of repentance is the moment of initiation. More than that: it is the means by which one alters one's past. The Greeks thought that impossible. They often say in their Gnomic aphorisms, 'Even the Gods cannot alter the past.' Christ showed that the commonest sinner could do it, that it was the one thing he could do. Christ, had he been asked, would have said—I feel quite certain about it—that the moment the prodigal son fell on his knees and wept, he made his having wasted his substance with harlots, his swineherding and hungering for the husks they ate, beautiful and holy moments in his life. It is difficult for most people to grasp the idea. I dare say one has to go to

> *The imagination is simply a manifestation of love.*

prison to understand it. If so, it may be worth while going to prison.

THERE is something so unique about Christ. Of course just as there are false dawns before the dawn itself, and winter days so full of sudden sunlight that they will cheat the wise crocus into squandering its gold before its time, and make some foolish bird call to its mate to build on barren boughs, so there were Christians before Christ. For that we should be grateful. The unfortunate thing is that there have been none since. I make one exception, St. Francis of Assisi. But then God had given him at his birth the soul of a poet, as he himself when quite young had in mystical marriage taken poverty as his bride: and with the soul of a poet and the body of a beggar he found the way to perfection not difficult. He understood Christ, and so he became like him. We do not require the *Liber Conformitatum* [Franciscan Rule of Order] to teach us that the life of St. Francis was the true *Imitatio Christi* [Imitation of Christ], a poem compared to which the book of that name is merely prose.

Indeed, that is the charm about Christ, when all is said: he is just like a work of art. He does not really teach one anything, but by being brought into his presence one becomes something. And everybody is predestined to his presence. Once at least in his life each man walks with Christ to Emmaus.

As regards the other subject, the Relation of the Artistic Life to Conduct, it will no doubt seem strange to you that I should select it. People point to Reading Gaol and say, 'That is where the artistic life leads a man.' Well, it might lead to worse places. The more mechanical people to whom life is a shrewd speculation depending on a careful calculation of ways and means, always know where they are going, and go there. They start with the ideal desire of being the parish beadle, and in whatever sphere they are placed they succeed in being the parish beadle and no more. A man whose desire is to be something separate from himself, to be a member of Parliament, or a successful grocer, or a prominent solicitor, or a judge, or something equally tedious, invariably succeeds in being what he wants to be. That is his punishment. Those who want a mask have to wear it.

> *Christ is just like a work of art. He does not really teach one anything, but by being brought into his presence one becomes something.*

But with the dynamic forces of life, and those in whom those dynamic forces become incarnate, it is different. People whose desire is solely for self-realization never know where they are going. They can't know. In one sense of the word it is of course necessary, as the Greek oracle said, to know oneself: that is the first achievement of knowledge. But to recognize that the soul of a man is unknowable, is the ultimate achievement of wisdom. The final mystery is oneself. When one has weighed the sun in the balance, and measured the steps of the moon, and mapped out the seven heavens star by star, there still remains oneself. Who can calculate the orbit of his own soul? When the son went out to look for his father's asses, he did not know that a man of God was waiting for him with the very chrism of coronation, and that his own soul was already the soul of a king.

I hope to live long enough and to produce work of such a character that I shall be able at the end of my days to say, 'Yes! this is just where the artistic life leads a man!' Two of the most perfect lives I have come across in my own experience are the lives of Verlaine and of Prince Kropotkin: both of them men who have passed years in prison: the first, the one Christian poet since Dante; the other, a man with a soul of that beautiful white Christ which seems coming out of Russia. And for the last seven or eight months, in spite of a succession of great troubles reaching me from the outside world almost without intermission, I have been placed in direct contact with a new spirit working in this prison through man and things, that has helped me beyond any possibility of expression in words: so that while for the first year of my imprisonment I did nothing else, and can remember doing nothing else, but wring my hands in impotent despair, and say, 'What an ending, what an appalling ending!' now I try to say to myself, and sometimes when I am not torturing myself do really and sincerely say, 'What a beginning, what a wonderful beginning!' It may really be so. It may become so. If it does I shall owe much to this new personality that has altered every man's life in this place.

> *To recognize that the soul of a man is unknowable, is the ultimate achievement of wisdom. The final mystery is oneself.*

You may realize it when I say that had I been released last May, as I tried to be, I would have left this place loathing it and every official in it with a bitterness of hatred that would have poisoned my life. I have had a year longer of imprisonment, but humanity has been in the prison along with us all, and now when I go out I shall always remember great kindnesses that I have received here from almost everybody, and on the day of my release I shall give many thanks to many people, and ask to be remembered by them in turn.

> *To have become a deeper man is the privilege of those who have suffered.*

The prison style is absolutely and entirely wrong. I would give anything to be able to alter it when I go out. I intend to try. But there is nothing in the world so wrong but that the spirit of humanity, which is the spirit of love, the spirit of the Christ who is not in churches, may make it, if not right, at least possible to be borne without too much bitterness of heart.

I know also that much is waiting for me outside that is very delightful, from what St. Francis of Assisi calls 'my brother the wind, and my sister the rain,' lovely things both of them, down to the shop-windows and sunsets of great cities. If I made a list of all that still remains to me, I don't know where I should stop: for, indeed, God made the world just as much for me as for anyone else. Perhaps I may go out with something that

I had not got before. I need not tell you that to me reformations in morals are as meaningless and vulgar as Reformations in theology. But while to propose to be a better man is a piece of unscientific cant, to have become a deeper man is the privilege of those who have suffered. And such I think I have become.

If after I am free a friend of mine gave a feast, and did not invite me to it, I should not mind a bit. I can be perfectly happy by myself. With freedom, flowers, books, and the moon, who could not be perfectly happy? Besides, feasts are not for me any more. I have given too many to care about them. That side of life is over for me, very fortunately, I dare say. But if after I am free a friend of mine had a sorrow and refused to allow me to share it, I should feel it most bitterly. If he shut the doors of the house of mourning against me, I would come back again and again and beg to be admitted, so that I might share in what I was entitled to share in. If he thought me unworthy, unfit to weep with him, I should feel it as the most poignant humiliation, as the most terrible mode in which disgrace could be inflicted on me. But that could not be. I have a right to share in sorrow, and he who can look at the loveliness of the world and share its sorrow, and realize something of the wonder of both, is in immediate contact with divine things, and has got as near to God's secret as anyone can get.

Perhaps there may come into my art also, no less than into my life, a still deeper note, one of greater unity of passion, and directness of impulse. Not width but intensity is the true aim of modern art. We are no longer in art concerned with the type. It is with the exception that we have to do. I cannot put my sufferings into any form they took, I need hardly say. Art only begins where Imitation ends, but something must come into my work, of fuller memory of words perhaps, of richer cadences, of more curious effects, of simpler architectural order, of some aesthetic quality at any rate.

When Marsyas was 'torn from the scabbard of his limbs'—*della vagina della membre sue*, to use one of Dante's most terrible Tacitean phrases—he had no more song, the Greek said. Apollo had been victor. The lyre had vanquished the reed. But perhaps the Greeks were mistaken. I hear in much modern Art the cry of Marsyas. It is bitter in Baudelaire, sweet and plaintive in Lamartine, mystic in Verlaine. It is in the deferred resolutions of Chopin's music. It is in the discontent that haunts Burne-Jones's women. Even Matthew Arnold, whose song of Callicles tells of 'the triumph of the sweet persuasive lyre,' and the 'famous final victory,' in such a clear note of lyrical beauty, has not a little of it; in the troubled undertone of doubt and distress that haunts his verses, neither Goethe nor Wordsworth could help him, though he followed each in turn, and when he seeks to mourn for *Thyrsis* or to sing of the *Scholar Gipsy*, it is the reed that he has to take for the rendering of his strain. But whether or not the Phrygian Faun was silent, I cannot be. Expression is as necessary to me as leaf and blossoms are to the black branches of the trees that show themselves above the prison walls and are so restless in the wind. Between my art and the world there is now a wide gulf, but between art and myself there is none. I hope at least that there is none.

> *He who can look at the loveliness of the world and share its sorrow, and realize something of the wonder of both . . . has got as near to God's secret as anyone can get.*

To each of us different fates are meted out. My lot has been one of public infamy, of long imprisonment, of misery, of ruin, of disgrace, but I am not worthy of it—not yet, at any rate. I remember that I used to say that I thought I could bear a real tragedy if it came to me with purple pall and a mask of noble sorrow, but that the dreadful thing about modernity was that it put tragedy into the raiment of comedy, so that the great realities seemed commonplace or grotesque or lacking in style. It is quite true about modernity. It has probably always been true about actual life. It is said that all martyrdoms seemed mean to the looker on. The nineteenth century is no exception to the rule.

Everything about my tragedy has been hideous, mean, repellent, lacking in style; our very dress makes us grotesque. We are the zanies of sorrow. We are clowns whose hearts are broken. We are specially designed to appeal to the sense of humor. On November 13th, 1895, I was brought down here from London. From two o'clock till half-past two on that day I had to stand on the centre platform of Clapham Junction in convict dress, and handcuffed, for the world to look at. I had been taken out of the hospital ward without a moment's notice being given to me. Of all possible objects I was the

> *A day in prison on which one does not weep is a day on which one's heart is hard, not a day on which one's heart is happy.*

most grotesque. When people saw me they laughed. Each train as it came up swelled the audience. Nothing could exceed their amusement. That was, of course, before they knew who I was. As soon as they had been informed they laughed still more. For half an hour I stood there in the grey November rain surrounded by a jeering mob.

For a year after that was done to me I wept every day at the same hour and for the same space of time. That is not such a tragic thing as possibly it sounds to you. To those who are in prison tears are a part of every day's experience. A day in prison on which one does not weep is a day on which one's heart is hard, not a day on which one's heart is happy.

> *Behind sorrow there is always a soul.*

Well, now I am really beginning to feel more regret for the people who laughed than for myself. Of course when they saw me I was not on my pedestal, I was in the pillory. But it is a very unimaginative nature that only cares for people on their pedestals. A pedestal may be a very unreal thing. A pillory is a terrific reality. They should have known also how to interpret sorrow better. I have said that behind sorrow there is always sorrow. It were wiser still to say that behind sorrow there is always a soul. And to mock at a soul in pain is a dreadful thing. In the strangely simple economy of the world people only get what they give, and to those who have not enough imagination to penetrate the mere outward of things, and feel pity, what pity can be given save that of scorn?

> *I can merely proceed on the lines of my own development, and, accepting all that has happened to me, make myself worthy of it.*

I write this account of the mode of my being transferred here simply that it should be realized how hard it has been for me to get anything out of my punishment but bitterness and despair. I have, however, to do it, and now and then I have moments of submission and acceptance. All the spring may be hidden in the single bud, and the low ground nest of the lark may hold the joy that is to herald the feet of many rose-red dawns. So perhaps whatever beauty of life still remains to me is contained in some moment of surrender, abasement, and humiliation. I can, at any rate, merely proceed on the lines of my own development, and, accepting all that has happened to me, make myself worthy of it.

People used to say of me that I was too individualistic. I must be far more of an individualist than ever I was. I must get far more out of myself than ever I got, and ask far less of the world than ever I asked. Indeed, my ruin came not from too great individualism of life, but from too little. The one disgraceful, unpardonable, and to all time contemptible action of my life was to allow myself to appeal to society for help and protection. To have made such an appeal would have been from the individualist point of view bad enough, but what excuse can there ever be put forward for having made it? Of course once I had put into motion the forces of society, society turned on me and said, 'Have you been living all this time in defiance of my laws, and do you now appeal to those laws for protection? You shall have those laws exercised to the full. You shall abide by what you have appealed to.' The result is I am in gaol. Certainly no man ever fell so ignobly, and by such ignoble instruments, as I did.

THE Philistine element in life is not the failure to understand art. Charming people, such as fishermen, shepherds, ploughboys, peasants and the like, know nothing about art, and are the very salt of the earth. He is the Philistine who upholds and aids the heavy, cumbrous, blind, mechanical forces of society, and who does not recognize dynamic force when he meets it either in a man or a movement.

People thought it dreadful of me to have entertained at dinner the evil things of life, and to have found pleasure in their company. But then, from the point of view through which I, as an artist in life, approach them they were delightfully suggestive and stimulating. The danger was half the excitement. My business as an artist was with Ariel. I set myself to wrestle with Caliban.

A great friend of mine—a friend of ten years' standing—came to see me some time ago, and told me that he did not believe a single word of what was said against me, and wished me to know that he considered me quite innocent, and the victim of a hideous plot. I burst into tears at what he said, and told him that while there was much amongst the definite charges that was quite untrue and transferred to me by revolting malice, still that my life had been full of perverse pleasures, and that unless he accepted that as a fact about me and realized it to the full I could not possibly be friends with him any more, or ever be in his company. It was a terrible shock to him, but we are friends, and I have not got his friendship on false pretenses.

Emotional forces, as I say somewhere in *Intentions*, are as limited in extent and duration as the forces of physical energy. The little cup that is made to hold so much can hold so much and no more, though all the purple vats of Burgundy be filled with wine to the brim, and the treaders stand knee-deep in the gathered grapes of the stony vineyards of Spain. There is no error more common than that of thinking that those who are the causes or occasions of great tragedies share in the feelings suitable to the tragic mood: no error more fatal than expecting it of them. The martyr in his 'shirt of flame' may be looking on the face of God, but to him who is piling the faggots or loosening the logs for the blast the whole scene is no more than the slaying of an ox is to the butcher, or the felling of a tree to the charcoal burner in the forest, or the fall of a flower to one who is mowing down the grass with a scythe. Great passions are for the great of soul, and great events can be seen only by those who are on a level with them.

> *Great passions are for the great of soul, and great events can be seen only by those who are on a level with them.*

I am to be released, if all goes well with me, towards the end of May, and hope to go at once to some little sea-side village abroad with Robbie and More Adey. The sea, as Euripides says in one of his plays about Iphigenia, washes away the stains and wounds of the world.

> *It seems to me that we all look at Nature too much, and live with her too little.*

I hope to be at least a month with my friends, and to gain peace and balance, and a less troubled heart, and a sweeter mood. I have a strange longing for the great simple primeval things, such as the sea, to me no less of a mother than the Earth. It seems to me that we all look at Nature too much, and live with her too little. I discern great sanity in the Greek attitude. They never chattered about sunsets, or discussed whether the shadows on the grass were really mauve or not. But they saw that the sea was for the swimmer, and the sand for the feet of the runner. They loved the trees for the shadow that they cast, and the forest for its silence at noon. The vineyard-dresser wreathed his hair with ivy that he might keep off the rays of the sun as he stooped over the young shoots, and for the artist and the athlete, the two types that Greece gave us, they plaited with garlands the leaves of the bitter laurel and of the wild parsley, which else had been of no service to men.

We call ours a utilitarian age, and we do not know the uses of any single thing. We have forgotten that water can cleanse, and fire purify, and that the Earth is mother to us all. As a consequence our art is of the moon and plays with shadows, while Greek art is of the sun and deals directly with things. I feel sure that in elemental forces there is purification, and I want to go back to them and live in their presence.

Of course to one so modern as I am, *'enfant de mon siècle'* [child of my century], merely to look at the world will be always lovely. I tremble with pleasure when I think that on the very day of my leaving prison both the laburnum and the lilac will be blooming in the gardens, and that I shall see the wind stir into restless beauty the swaying gold of the one, and make the other toss the pale purple of its plumes, so that all the air shall be Arabia for me. Linnaeus fell on his knees and wept for joy when he saw for the first time the long heath of some English upland made yellow with the tawny aromatic brooms of the common furze; and I know that for me, to whom flowers are part of desire,

> **We have forgotten that water can cleanse, and fire purify, and that the Earth is mother to us all.**

there are tears waiting in the petals of some rose. It has always been so with me from my boyhood. There is not a single color hidden away in the chalice of a flower, or the curve of a shell, to which, by some subtle sympathy with the very soul of things, my nature does not answer. Like Gautier, I have always been one of those '*pour qui le monde visible existe*' [for whom the visible world exists].

Still, I am conscious now that behind all this beauty, satisfying though it may be, there is some spirit hidden of which the painted forms and shapes are but modes of manifestation, and it is with this spirit that I desire to become in harmony. I have grown tired of the articulate utterances of men and things. The Mystical in Art, the Mystical in Life, the Mystical in Nature; this is what I am looking for, and in the great symphonies of music, in the initiation of sorrow, in the depths of the sea, I may find it. It is absolutely necessary for me to find it somewhere.

All trials are trials for one's life, just as all sentences are sentences of death; and three times have I been tried.

The first time I left the box to be arrested, the second time to be led back to the house of detention, the third time to pass into a prison for two years. Society, as we have constituted it, will have no place for me, has none to offer; but Nature, whose sweet rains fall on unjust and just alike, will have clefts in the rocks where I may hide, and secret valleys in whose silence I may weep undisturbed. She will hang the night with stars so that I may walk abroad in the darkness without stumbling, and send the wind over my footprints so that none may track me to my hurt: she will cleanse me in great waters, and with bitter herbs make me whole.

> *The past, the present, and the future are but one moment in the sight of God, in whose sight we should try to live.*

Do not be afraid of the past. When people say that it is irrevocable, do not believe them. The past, the present, and the future are but one moment in the sight of God, in whose sight we should try to live. Time and space, succession and extension, are merely accidental conditions of thought. The imagination can transcend them and move in a free sphere of ideal existences.

Things, also, are in their essence what we choose to make them. A thing *is*, according to the mode at which one looks at it. 'Where others see but the dawn coming over the hill, I see the sons of God shouting for joy.'

What seemed to the world and to myself my future I lost irretrievably when I went to prison. Really, I daresay, I had lost it long before that. What lies before me is my past. I have got to make myself look on that with different eyes, to make the world look on it with different eyes, to make God look on it with different eyes. This I cannot do by ignoring it, or slighting it, or praising it, or denying it. It is only to be done by fully accepting it as an inevitable part of the evolution of my life and character, by bowing my head to everything that I have suffered.

Incomplete, imperfect as I am, yet I still have much to give. People came to me to learn the Pleasure of Life and the Pleasure of Art. Perhaps I am chosen to teach something much more wonderful:

> THE MEANING OF SORROW,
> AND ITS BEAUTY.

FURTHER READING

As a Man Thinketh
the wisdom of JAMES ALLEN

THE MANUAL
A Philosopher's Guide to Life
EPICTETUS

THE MEDITATIONS
An Emperor's Guide to Mastery
MARCUS AURELIUS

EVERYDAY EMERSON
THE WISDOM OF RALPH WALDO EMERSON
PARAPHRASED BY SAM TORODE

www.amazon.com/author/samtorode

Made in the USA
San Bernardino, CA
09 May 2018